www.Rrobertwarren.com

The first 10,000 copies sold will benefit the

501©3 not-for-profit
MidCity Excellence

Community Learning Center:

www.visitmce.org

A Book of Poems and Prayers for the Most Difficult Times in Life

www.rrobertwarren.com
www.visitmce.org
www.visitwordoffaith.com
www.americangrantservice.com

Photos by: Sharyn Sanders
www.seraphimstudios.net

Other photo contributions by:
Angela Alford (page 75)   Kimberly Warren & Robert Foster (page 91)
R. Robert Warren, Jr. (pages 19, 45, 63, 68, 69, 70, 71, 81, 89, 109)

Cover Designs: Kimberly Y. Warren & the American Grant Writing Firm,
Inc. **www.americangrantservice.com**

Editors: Cozetta M. Foster & Kimberly Y. Warren

Scripture quotations are from the King James Version of the Holy Bible
unless otherwise noted.

United States Copyright Office
Library of Congress Cataloging-in-Publication
Data- A Book of Poems and Prayers for the Most Difficult
Times in Life

Indexing: Literary Work
**Library of Congress Control (LCCN)# 1-644286161
20110804_202024 Psalm of David
ISBN# 978-0-615-54383-3**

Printed in the United States of America- Amazon.com

www.rrobertwarren.com

A Book of Poems & Prayers

For The Most *Difficult* Times In Life

By R. Robert Warren Jr., MS Ed.
www.rrobertwarren.com

Photos by: Sharyn Sanders, B.S.
www.seraphimstudios.net

Contents

www.rrobertwarren.com

BOOK DEDICATION

To My Beloved Wife- Kimberly Y. Warren

Love's Patient

As a snowball sits on a window pain,
First comes the cloud, then comes the rain.
As a ladle in hand idle and still,
First comes the bucket for water to fill.
As a cool breath of water when sent from above,
First comes the bosom, then comes the love.

PREFACE

This Inspirational Book is Food for the Soul!

Because our imperfect world is inhabited with imperfect human beings- at one point in life we will all face a battle that is seemingly beyond our control. While the situations, places, names and faces change- we will often see a reoccurring theme of anxiety, depression, confusion and pain. Many writers of The Holy Bible experienced both depressing lows and joyous highs. Poet and Song Writer, King David wrote in Psalms 56:8 (English Standard Version):

[8]You have kept count of my tossings;
  put my tears in your bottle.
  Are they not in your book?
[9]Then my enemies will turn back
  in the day when I call.
  This I know, that God is for me.
[10]In God, whose word I praise,
  in the LORD, whose word I praise,
[11]in God I trust; I shall not be afraid.
  What can man do to me?

Each experience is unique as we struggle in the vicissitudes of life: though it be cancer, heart failure, diseases of every nature, accidents, trauma, violence, broken promise, shattered dreams, financial and emotional bankruptcy and sometimes death.

Sometimes we measure the catastrophic loss like a tornado or hurricane and some carry the hurt as a lifetime badge of honor as we share stories gauging whose tragedy seems to be the greatest. But no matter what the challenge- no matter the agony or turmoil- the final summation is that pain is pain- is pain- is pain. But thanks be to God it does not conclude there. There is rest for weary souls and hope that we can become better, not bitter because of the struggle.

But- the old adage that "misery loves company" is *not* why this book was authored. This is an attempt to unashamedly bare my soul as I struggled to find resolution and solace and proactively confront conflicts of life. Indeed- **A Book of Poems and Prayers for the Most Difficult Times in Life** is more than a literary work! You will come to understand how I faced traumatic situations & troublesome times: survived 6 family deaths in 2009; addressed economic pressures of founding an inner city ministry mentoring at-risk youth in 150 year old dilapidated buildings, on an at-risk shoe-string budget & just challenging everyday hardships of life! This is indeed an inspirational work that spans 25 years of life, death, failures and successes.

In 45 poetic cries and declarations, it was my intent to help even the most desperate individual begin the healing process, bringing resolve, enlightenment and hope.

* Read it to comfort someone who is grieving, Hospitalized or has just experienced a loss.
* Discuss it at a book club or support group to facilitate thought-provoking discourse.
* Listen to it on CD for a morning devotion or afternoon tea.
* Study it for love, loss, death and life!

We pray that you will be inspired!

Websites: www.rrobertwarren.com
www.visitmce.org   www.americangrantservice.com

Contact: 604 S 20th St. St. Joseph, MO 64507
Ph.#: 816. 294.8936 or 816.294.4727
Email: *rrobertwr@aol.com or visitmce@gmail.com*

SECTION I: NATURE

To Touch The Sky

To reach for the stars is great;

But if I may but touch the skies,

Then my living will not be in vain.

Then my song will become a symphony,

The river, an ocean of love -

That which is dead will come alive again.

Teach me oh Lord to number my days;

To give glory to You now,

And praise forever in The Next.

By R. Robert Warren, Jr.

PERFECT PEACE

In the quiet stillness and

dark of night.

In the cold wet clenches

of nights winter,

There, I have found my peace.

This has become my Valley Forge,

This has become my darkest

before dawn.

This has become my Festival of Lights,

The flight of swift men,

and knobs of light.

In the quiet stillness and dark of night,

In the cold wet clenches

of winter's fleece.

THERE I HAVE FOUND,

THERE I HAVE FOUND,

THERE I HAVE FOUND...

MY PERFECT PEACE.

THE SUNRISE

Come away sun.

Rise above the dark

clouds of the night.

Pierce through the darkness...

And shine

again.

SECTION II: SONGS

HOLY SPIRIT YOU ARE WELCOME

Holy Spirit,

You are welcome

Holy Spirit,

You are welcome.

Come

and fill the breaches of my soul.

Cleanse me...

make me whole.

SHEKINAH GLORY

There is a river flowing near,
and I can take you, can take you there.
Cross over, Cross over, Cross over & see.
Shekinah glory, Shekinah grace,
Shekinah glory, Shekinah grace.

There is a sea, a sea of glass
as clear as crystal that few can pass.
Cross over, Cross over, Cross over & see.
Shekinah glory, Shekinah grace,
Shekinah glory, Shekinah grace.

There is a throne with majesty,
and oh the face, the face I see,
Cross over, Cross over, Cross over & see.
Shekinah glory, Shekinah grace,
Shekinah glory,
Shekinah...
Grace...

Keep Patiently Waiting

Life at its best is just a fleeting vapor,

Whirling and twirling until it comes to an end.

And I'm in the middle of this endless cycle,

Hoping... praying for a chance for me to win.

But then he comes and tells me so,

Keep patiently waiting and you will know.

Yes, Jesus comes and tells me so,

Keep patiently waiting and you will know.

Hold out when the going gets tough,

Keeping the faith when the going gets rough.

Yes, Hold out when the going gets tough,

Just keeping the faith when the going gets rough.

But then he comes and tells me so,

Keep patiently waiting and you will know.

Yes, Jesus comes and tells me so,

Keep patiently waiting and you will know.

STREET CRIES

Dear Jesus, I've got something to say,
I've tried to talk before but...
couldn't find the words to say.
Cryin' in the mornin' tears late at night,
Tell me how long can I fake this game,
there's just no end in sight.

See I tried to tell my mother, my father I never knew,
That's why I thought I'd come before ya',
and try to tell you.
You see life's, so hard, my mind so far,
That's why I gotta' say it, say it,
Say it, Say it,
Say it- I surrender.

See I've tried, so hard,
to do it on my own,
And I tried to save my self
but I don't know,
I don't know, I don't know,
don't know how.

Gotta' call the other day,
from one of my friends,
So caught up in the game,
I fear he has no end.
Come and Save Me, Save Me,
Save Me,
Save...

GOLGOTHA ROAD

When it seems that I've come to the end of my road,
And all life seems in vain,
Though all I have is in me- I can not see my way.
So I must go 'cause moving helps my pain.

So here I go back down that Golgotha road again
Without a doubt, and there's no fear within.
And one thing I know for sure, I travel not alone,
For there was one who traveled it for me.

When it seems that I've come to the end of my road,
And all my friends have 'turned their back on me',
Yet I can not fight this road my feet are set upon,
So I must go, 'cause there's more he has for me.

So here I go back down that Golgotha road again
Without a doubt, and there's no fear within.
And one thing I know for sure, I travel not alone,
For there was one who traveled it for me.

It's the hill of Calvary, the road of suffering,
So I gotta' go 'cause he bore that cross for me.
So here I go back down that Golgotha road again
Without a doubt, and there's no fear within.

And one thing I know for sure, I travel not alone,
For there was one who traveled it for ME
And the more and more I travel, it all makes sense to me;
That I'm traveling this road...to be free.

I Just Want to Be Close To You

Verse 1:
Trials come to block my path,
Trials go, see they don't last.
Just when it seems that it's over and done,
Another one comes to pass.
That's when I say:

Chorus:
Things done wrong, I just want to do right,
Things done wrong, I just want to live right –
I just want to be close to You, JESUS,
I just want to be close to You.

Verse 2:
There are times when I feel so alone,
There are times, when my mind comes and goes.
Just when I'm about to throw my hands up,
Your love shines through all my clouds.
That when I say:

Chorus:
Things done wrong, I just want to do right,
Things done wrong, I just want to live right –
I just want to be close to You, JESUS,
I just want to be close to You.

SECTION III: DEATH & LIFE

*(Death: Consists of a set of poems written when a lily in the valley- my **Aunt Lillie Mae Reed**- passed away)*

DEATH I

TURN BACK TIME

OH LORD,

TURN BACK THE HANDS OF TIME,

REMOVE DEATH FAR FROM ME.

THOUGH MY BONES ARE FRAIL

AND LIFE HAS SLIPPED FROM MY TORSO,

YET IN YOU WILL I PUT MY TRUST.

AND YES, OH GOD, I KNOW

THAT MY SOUL IS READY TO MEET YOU,

AND MY HEART LONGS TO SEE YOU;

BUT, FOR MY CHILDREN'S SAKE,

TURN BACK TIME,

TURN BACK...

TURN.

DEATH II

THE DANCE OF DEATH

DEATH DANCED AND DANCED

AND DANCED AGAIN,

HE SAW AN OPENING IN THE WIND.

AH HAA, HE SAID TO HER-

I GO TO DANCE MY DANCE,

MAKE HER MY FOE.

FASTER AND FASTER I'M ALMOST THERE,

I CAN SEE THE DOOR: THE KEYS OF FEAR.

OH NO! NOT AGAIN,

NOT AGAIN, AGAIN;

PRAYER HAS STOPPED MY FORWARD REIGN.

UNTIL THE NEXT, TIME I'LL BE,

AND DANCE MY DANCE SO VIVIDLY, DANCE!

DEATH III

DEATH STOPS

DEATH STOPPED ON THE ROAD THIS DAY,

AND CARRIED ME ALONG THE WAY.

HIS GRIM FACE AND PIERCING EYES

THOUGH NOT A FEAR WITHIN ME LIES.

FOR THIS I KNOW OF WHOM I STAND,

THE STING OF DEATH CANNOT ME GLANCE.

THE MESSIAH'S CALL TOO DEEP WITHIN,

MY SWORD LAID DOWN; I REST NOW…

THE END.

LIFE I

I have but one heart, one soul, one life.

How dark it is,

nothing anywhere to be seen.

Yet I am reminded to continue on,

Stand my ground, keep my rank.

But the feeling of anguish is upon me,

Who can know it but I?

Life... continues.

LIFE II

I saw a light in the sky,

How wondrous and beautiful it was.

I followed it forever;

Yet the closer I got,

the further it went from me.

So I ran and I ran,

stumbling yet pushing.

Until at last the earth I could not see.

Then suddenly it was upon me!

How glorious yet dreadful to see it.

Aah. Life...has ceased.

LIFE III

Still small voices

ringing through my head

Stop shoving, stop pushing,

slow down instead.

For the race is not swift,

nor the battle one of rage,

But timing, timing,

and little drops of age.

A still small voice I hear,

"Look for me instead" -

For I will be the one,

with victory on my head.

Life...is time!

SECTION IV: HONOR & GLORY TO GOD

The Living Way

Abraham!

The goat, the ram,

The dove, the bull;

A smoking burning lamp,

Upon the highest point it lay.

But Oh the glory in the distance,

Before the world was made

Jesus Christ, the new...

Aah, The Living Way.

International Award Winning Poem-
1st Place for the PAW, Inc. Convention

The Glory's Here

I never knew the radiant glory; I kept passing by,

And never told the story.

I tried to do it but it never came out,

But then I got stuck so now I only shout.

I shout from the roof tops I shout from the grave,

I shout from the stars the endless raves.

The Glory's Here! The Glory's Here!

Come near and come far for The Glory is Here.

Now I pass by and not afraid to walk in,

Oh it's so radiant, Oh it so mends.

I never saw it like this; I never saw it before,

The doors now open, step in,

Aaah... MORE.

PERFECT PEACE

THANK YOU, OH GOD

I see, Lord, I see.
You thought you could
Hide it from me
But I understand.
God's thoughts I have not
But the mind of Christ I have.

I saw it in prayer one day;
Plus, time had much to do with it –
Just waiting patiently,
As you worked out
All the smallest details.

Thank you, oh God, Thank you!
You showed me much,
And for that I'm grateful.
Prayer has allowed
Me to see beyond
This present time and pain.

Thank you, oh God,
Thank You.

BE STILL

Be still and oh so silent,
Shhh, and say no more.
All around is glory, precious glory.
Angelic host flapping their wings
As life in slow motion

Or the rush of willow trees,
"swoosh, swoosh".
Oh be still and oh so silent.
For this is the glory of the Lord,
And this is none other than the spirit of life itself.

My flesh melts
in the presence of this radiance.
This is awesome,
so awesome,
"swoosh, swoosh".

Be still and oh so silent,
for this is the glory of The Lord,
and none other than the spirit of life itself.

The voice cries "Come up hither my son,
for as I have pulled you out of your own muck
and mire so will I pull you out of this grave danger."

Be still and oh so silent,
for this is the glory of The Lord,
and none other than the spirit of life itself.

TO KNOW THE MAKER

Of love and laughter,
of joy and pain,
The one loves all,
the other maims.

Of rhyme and rhymeric,
the sweetest songs,
Whether good or bad,
to someone belongs.

Of life and liberty,
of tragedy and grief,
Yet around them all
a simple reef.

The bond of truth,
unsnapped or crushed,
The simplest light
of a babies touch.

Of children's laughter
the greatest games,
Aaah the sounds,
so unrestrained

But the greatest of all,
direst or sane,
Is to know the Maker,
and know His name.

BE FREE

Oh God, my God, how Magnificent is your name.
How wonderful are Your works to behold.
Today I have seen Your mighty acts,
The glorious working of Power and deliverance.

And though I am Not totally free, yet I am free –
The cloud of darkness, The cloud of debt lifted.
Aaah, and now I hear The Voice, That still small voice so clear,
And yet, so far away Speaking words so dear to me:

The truth, the truth Has not yet been seen,
Neither have the clouds of brightness been revealed.
Yes, yes, oh man of God, You are delivered & you are free.
Speak no more of this – For your eyes have seen my glory!

Debt has passed over
And the struggle shall be no more.
Be Free man of God,
Be Free...

SECTION V: FAMILY

RAY

I'm strong as an ox, with a laugh like a clown,
But known as "Preacha Warren" in a small little town.
I drove the school bus, and was custodian you see,
Why I even was president of NAACP.

With a little ole' church way out in the woods,
Outhouses for rest rooms, if that can be understood.
I tried to raise hogs, and chickens and hens,
But those darn animals wouldn't stay in their pens.

The hogs climbed the fence, the chickens flew about,
No matter what I did, they just kept gettin' out.
So I gave that up, and left it alone,
But I kept right on preachin' 'cause that was my home.

I preached in small towns where no one would go,
Had to do "The Lawd's" work, so everyone could know.
I drove all my kids, see they were my choir,
Had to give them a heart, for The Lord's desire.

In the summer I'd rest, bean poles just startin',
Kids runnin' 'round, "Hey! Get outta" 'dat garden!"
I'd preach and I'd preach, 'til they all started moanin'
Boy, I could hear it now, eleven o' clock in the morning.

"When you talkin' about Jesus, He's a friend of mine"
But I'd keep right on preachin' 'til the "Bread & the Wine".
And as I got older, though I wasn't surprised,
My son started preachin, in front of my eyes.

The fire of his daddy, his mother's heart in his chest,
Yea, I got to see it all, b'fore I took my last breath.
Now I can rest, with that same thought in mind,
'Cause I've laid down my sword…for the very last time.

Dedicated my Father: Rev. Rayphell Warren, Sr.
"Love You Daddy"

RUTH

I'm a survivor!
Through tough times, through rough times,
Sad times, and bad times, I'm a survivor.
My hands have held a wooden plow,
So that my father could wipe his brow.

Pulling and toiling behind a mule,
Keeping it straight, and doing my best,
So that my father could have a rest.
Keeping my younger siblings in line,
See that's how it was, back in them times.

My eyes have watched a bleeding son;
The sound of an ambulance, a drunk- hit and run.
The blood unstoppable, a flat tire on the way,
A two and half-hour drive – impossible to say.

But I held fast to the WORD, Ezekiel Sixteen,
Repeating it over – had faith to believe.
"When I saw thee polluted in thy blood",
I read without doubting,
Then all of a sudden, the bleeding stopped spouting.

My feet have stood at the bed of the dying,
My father, my mother, my niece and my brother;
A rock of strength when they needed it most,
But that was my call, I have nothing to boast.

The loss of a husband, feeling alone,
But I'm not afraid, my God's on the throne.
The Bright and Morning Star shines high above,
Extending his arms and power of love.

My mouth has spoken the unchangeable WORD,
Teaching's *my* call, so it could be heard.
My nose has smelled my famous peach cobbler,
Home-made cake and caramel icing gobblers.

Yes, I'm a survivor; I cannot tell it all,
'Cause my son wrote this poem, see that's *his* call.

Dedicated my Mother: Ruth A. Warren "Love You Mama"

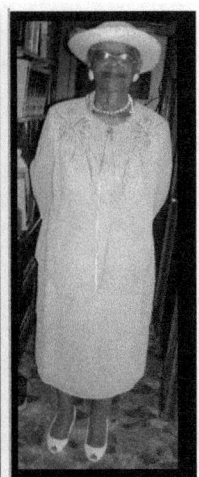

The Four Leaf Clover

Hang in there mom
it's almost over,
Our God's more than
a four leaf clover.

Through anguish of mind,
and terrible shakes,
Am I going the wrong way,
did I make a mistake?

Aah but I'm strong as an anvil,
as quick as a snake,
I'll strengthen my arms,
I'll pray 'til it aches.

But what of my youth,
what of my song,
How can I write
when *my* strength is gone?

I've gone over and over,
and over again,
I just can't find it,
can't find any sin.

Aah, then
it must be you devil,
you caused all this grief,
But I'll fight and I'll fight
'til I find the relief.

My faith is strong, and my eye is not dim,
My God shall arise, my faith is in Him.
So rise oh Lord, let your enemies be scattered,
This sickness can't hold me, though I'm torn and I'm battered.

Cancer!? Ah Ha, what is that to The Lord?
He'll blow with one breath, and it's gone with his sword.
Aah but the cost, the cost, how can I stay?
So much to fight, and so much to pay.

But through it all I'm learning, my strength is in Christ,
So get back doubt, 'cause *He's* paid the price.
I'll keep up the fight and I'll hang right in,
For Christ paid it all, for me, and for sin.

With every stripe on his back, every bruise on His knee;
So thank you Lord Jesus, 'cause It could have been me.
My faith is stronger than it's ever been,
And if I had to do it over, I'd do it again.

Hang in there mom it's almost over,
Our God's more than a four leaf clover.

Dedicated to my Mother-in-Love: Lady Cozetta M. Foster in her fight with cancer.

73

FOR THAT HE WAS MADE

Quick and Witty
a counselor by trade,
But radical for Christ,
for that he was made.

Tried and tested
as faithful as stone,
Out running them all
with a style all his own.

Raised all his children
with caution and poise,
But not afraid to tell 'em,
"Gotta' watch 'em all boy!"

So preach on Dad
fight the good fight of faith,
Shake every devil
and rip every snake.

Preach down heaven;
make 'em all shout,
For thy light, Man of God,
shall never go out.

And when it's all over –
a long race you will run,
You'll look back and say,
"For Christ it was done".

Quick and Witty
a counselor by trade,
But radical for Christ,
for that he was made.

Dedicated to my Father-in-Love
Pastor James P. Foster Jr.

SECTION VI: PATRIOTIC

AMERICA

MY COUNTRY 'TIS OF THEE,
TRULY THE LAND OF LIBERTY.
THOUGH AS THE FALL OF ROME IT SEEMS,
AS THORNS AND THISTLES GATHER,
AND 'TEND TO SWALLOW THEE.
YET OUT OF THEE SHALL COME
A DELIVERER SO GREAT,
AN ANCIENT ONE, TO TURN YOUR FATE -
TO LEAD WITH VIGOR & LOVE NOT HATE.

YET IN THE END WITH ALL THE NATIONS,
THE FIG TREE YOU'LL GATHER 'ROUND,
AND FIX YOUR BOWS WITH FORCE UNBOUND.
AWE, BUT IF YOU KNEW THE HUSBANDMAN,
WHO HIDES BEHINDS THE VINE,
YOU'D STAY AT HOME, YEA ALL THE NATIONS,
FOR ONLY HE CAN SHINE.

BUT AS FOR NOW GAIN STRENGTH;
FOR THERE ARE MANY DAYS AHEAD,
BEFORE THIS DOOM AND PAINFUL DREAD.
AND LEAD WITH STRENGTH,
YEA GATHER SPOIL,
FOR GOD IS WITH THEE,
THROUGH ALL THIS TOIL.

THE SOLDIER

Yes, I carried you
when you were young
But, I have carried you long enough
I have held the hand,
clasp the fingers,
strengthened the arm.

Yet, now shall you bear
your own burden,
the weight on your
own shoulder,
The cross on your own back –
Fall in line.

For these are the days
of vengeance,
Death, anger and violence.
I can carry you no longer.

Sergeant/Bishop
James P. Foster, Sr.
& Lady Gloria Foster

The shoulders
now made strong,
awe the eyes sharp
as a razor –
piercing with light.

Let us go soldier,
Let us march
for the battle ahead.

SECTION VII: TROUBLE & TRIUMPH

THE ENEMY

SILENT!
Be still.
Piercing red eyes,
Creeping things,
and gross darkness all around.

Aaah,
you are the one
whom the enemy has sent to dishonor,
and block my path.

With the flick of one finger,
and so is he gone.

The light springs forth...
and all
is
well.

LOOK BEYOND

Look beyond. Look beyond.
I've heard the tramping of the enemy,
The whistling of the arrows sailing by and by.
"Aw- you deserve this, you deserve to die."

Look beyond, look beyond,
Beyond the fall, beyond the pain;
Beyond the horses, the horses reins.
Galloping fiercely, galloping free,

Trying to catch me, trying to see.
To see if I've faltered, to see if I've failed,
But I've looked beyond that stinking pale.
So look beyond, look beyond and see
Aaah the race...was won for me.
LOOK BEYOND!

YET THERE IS NO END

It is evening Lord, and yet
there is no end of the work that must be done.
Another work, another device,
another grinding of the hands,
Another ministry,
And yet, there is no end.
Where shall I find the time, where the space;
Infinity is only ahead,
and yet there is no end.
The family calling, the dog barking,
The ratta-tat-tat of a worker on another job,
and yet there is no end. No end... no end.
Yet... far beyond infinity,
If there be such a thing, there is hope!
I've heard of such a place,
but I never thought, I... never thought.
Yes! There it is, there it is... there it is.
I can do this now, it's not about me.
Let the family cry, the dog bark,
the tat of another worker go on. For now I get it.
Far, far, far, beyond infinity I see it;
it was there all the time.
There is an end; there is an end, an end;
It's not about me.
Come... Let us march on.

'Cause I've Got M' Stuff!!

OH the dark places that I have been,
The snow covered benches the shivering skin.

And the thing that's so funny
the thing that's so true,
Is the light was there through all that blue.

Now winter has passed and the light now burns,
I found the soft touches of life's simple turns.

It seemed so long, the road so tough,
But it's over now, Press on, Sing, Praise...
'Cause "I've - got - m' - STUFF!!"

I DON'T UNDERSTAND

I don't understand the master's plan,
To scrimp and scrape and still not stand?
No light, no life, nothing at end?
How long must I endure this pestilence of life – it - self?

Oh yes I know, stand strong, stand tall,
Man, God will catch the greatest fall.
Curses! Curses!
I've heard it all before, I've heard it all before...
Oh yes, I've heard it ALL!
NO, NO, NO! I will not look at the light!
NO, NO, I will not look!

But, oh my Father,
I know that in you there is no darkness.
I don't understand and cannot see,
But thou seest all the smallest thing.
Forgive me Lord, cast me not away.
I'll stand, I'll stay, give it all away.
And scrimp and scrape and barely stand,
Though the master's call... I don't understand.

THE END IS NEAR

OH GOD, MY GOD, HOW LONG? How long must we wait ere the light of truth and deliverance from this debt be paid?

We have grappled and fussed 'til there is no strength left; Joy is gone and there is no light. Deliver us Oh God from the jaws of this slave master.

He has ripped and torn, snarled and laughed, howled and hooted 'til life itself has left. Curse him! Curse him!! May death, consume him! This very hour is just...just...

Yet, Look! Aaah yes, there is a glimmer of hope; the light through the tunnel awaits. "Come on, Come on" he says; the end is near. Crawl, walk, whatever you must do but don't – give – up.

The end is near, the end is near. Aaah yes, the end IS NEAR!

GO DOWN
AND
WAIT

Go down
and
wait.

There is a small ray
of light

Just over
the tree tops.

Go down...
wait,

And follow
your dreams.

THE LIGHT AT THE END

Have you ever seen a light
that you could not reach?
So far it seems
beyond the breach.

The closer you get
the further it goes,
But don't worry my friend,
it's still there, it knows.

I say "IT",
because "IT" really is true,
There is a light,
at the end of you.

The Smallest Trees

Isn't it amazing that the greatest thing we want,
Hides behind the smallest trees.
We look, and we look, at the forest beyond,
Only to find nothing at all.
Is it here, is it there? Oh it must be this tree.
For what I'm looking for is so great, so huge,
It must be the greatest, tree so tall.
But we look, and we look, and find nothing at all.

Then we get mad, we get angry;
Why God, why God, why God why,
I cannot find it, is it in the Sky?
Then we throw a temper tantrum,
We kick and we scream,
hoping to get His attention;
Only to hear, "Not that one, not that either,
That's not it, but good intentions."

Then we fold our hands and we say,
"Looky here you see,
I'm just not gonna' find it, he took it from me!"
But then we gently hear His voice so still,
"Look again, look again,
it's in my will."
Then we patiently wait, we patiently look,
For the Master said, it's in His book.

Then all of a sudden... I just couldn't have imagined;
This tree, this tree, this tree this,
No wonder, no wonder, no wonder I missed.
Far, far in the distance, where I couldn't see,
There was this little, little tree you see.
So small and insignificant, no meaning at all,
But when I looked behind it.....

Wow! I just couldn't have imagined...
How? How could I have missed it?
Covered by the leaves, covered by the snow,
Hid what I was looking for, looking for ya' know.

Oooh, but what I learned through all of this,
It was RIGHT HERE, RIGHT HERE, can't believe I missed.
That's why I said; whiles I get some ZZZZZZ's,
The greatest thing hides... behind the smallest trees.

How Lofty Are The Trees

Oh how lofty are the trees,
The daffodils – leaves
Swaying in the wind.
Take flight oh my soul take flight;

Turn the emptiness of my heart into Joy again
May my dark days, see brighter tomorrows.
Oh that my soul would take flight
As the blowing leaves.

Oh that my joy would give praise
As the swaying limbs.
Oh that I could find rest in the night:
Like the dew on the morning leaf.

OH that I could laugh again, HA, HA, HA!
Oh how lofty are the trees,
And my soul... Aah, now finds rest,
In Thy WORD.

Moving Is Better Than Standing Still

Two stars sit in yonder sky,
Ere I saw them not I know not why.
For my head was down and feeling low,
As I thought upon the things of woe.

But then I stopped and looked upon,
The luscious hills of the vast beyond.
Then I saw the stars so bright,
The one on the left, the other right.

I thought how marvelous
and wondrous it must be,
To sit so high above the trees.
So I stopped again and wondered why,
Why not stay beneath this sky?

With my soul so vexed, compressed and down,
What would it hurt to stay on this ground?
But, then I said I cannot stay,
For there are too many lessons along the way.

And who's to say what life will fill,
The cracks and crevasses with life's mending mill.
So I'll keep moving, and won't look back,
For there's a power beyond the stars, a fact.

And see what lies o'er yonder hill,
For moving is better…than standing still.

THE MOON AWAITS

The moon awaits as the sun sets,
To show itself strong,
and have no regrets.

So come away oh moon,
Shine through the lining of the clouds.
Pierce through the darkness,
And give us light.

What Is Light

What is light, and what is darkness?
And what if the light at the end of the tunnel cease?
Can I but see the power of which I fight?
Can I but see the power that rages?
That within me boils, that cause the burn?

Aah, the fog of night,
so dark that one cannot see the hand.
And what of thee oh moon, can you not come out?
Can the clouds not move, can the fog not lift?
Can the wind not blow? BE STILL!!

Aah, and no sense of the day, nor twilight, nor dawn.
And what of thee oh sun,
Cannot thy rays burn away the darkness?
Can you not cast out the clouds with heat?
But now day is night, and night is day,
And how dark is the night.

Arrgh! The anger boils, Arrgh! The fire rages.
Aah, what of the end?
THIS IS NOT FAIR, I SAY, THIS IS NOT FAIR!

Yet, I've heard that He who passes by,
slumbers not nor sleeps.
He walks in the midst of the darkness,
and cools the fires of night.
He brings light to the clouds of night,
and lifts the fog about.
He gently speaks to my spirit within,
and calms my inner rage.

And though the darkness is without,
yet there is light within.

So come thy way oh darkness,
come thy way oh fog of night.
For I see through thee oh sea of darkness,
And thy vast doors of death have been closed.

For light has sprung and I, yes I...can see again.
In thee oh LORD I put my trust,
May I never, doubt you again!

About the Author
(Biography)

R. Robert "Buster" Warren, Jr., MS Ed. began his life as a preacher's kid and the youngest of 7 children growing up just outside Poplar Bluff, MO in the Providence/ Morocco community.

As a young boy he learned to drive on a tractor and graduated at Poplar Bluff High School with a perfect attendance- never missing a day of school during his K-12th grade years. He gained strong work ethics from his family of African American farmers, attending New Home Missionary Baptist Church, once pastored by Rev. Rayphell Warren, Sr. (mother- Mrs. Ruth A. Warren).

In 1984, Pastor Warren attended Missouri Western State University with a unique combination of football and vocal music scholarships. After graduating with a bachelor's in Music Education, he married his wife, Kimberly (Foster) Warren in 1992. In 2000, he founded the Word of Faith Family Worship Center located on 20th & Messanie in St. Joseph, MO. Pastor Robert also taught vocal and instrumental music professionally and coached football for 10 years at public and private schools.

After he and his wife graduated with their Masters in Education in 2001, they founded a community learning center, MidCity Excellence that serves youth, adults/seniors annually in the performing arts & dance center, computer training, leadership and family programs.

The community mission, currently trains men and women in leadership, conflict resolution and spiritual development; providing direction, hope & purpose through mentoring ex-offenders and men in their "Man-Up" Initiative and also by reaching the youth in the life center. This non-profit 501©3 engages families in fitness activities, career development, praise dance/step teams ("Sons of Thunder" and "Inspirational Angels") and academic support/tutoring.

Pastor Warren has served on the Allied Arts Council Board of Directors, loves to sing with the St. Joseph Community Chorus and was one of Colin Powell's AmeriCorps Promise Fellows. He hopes to pursue a Doctorate in Education Administration in the near future.

Hobbies: Singing opera, bike riding, weightlifting, playing pool and studying religious and ancient history.

Word of Faith Family Worship Center

CONTACT:

Pastor R. Robert Warren, Jr., MS Ed. is available for conferences, motivational speaking, workshops, book clubs, poetry readings & preaching engagements.

www.RROBERTWARREN.COM
Office: 604 S 20th St St. Joseph, MO 64507
Ph.#:   816.294.8936 or 816.294.4727
Email: visitmce@gmail.com or
      rrobertwr@aol.com

To learn more about our non-profit community learning center or other ventures- please visit our websites:

www.rrobertwarren.com
www.visitmce.org
www.americangrantservice.com
www.visitwordoffaith.com

CONTACT:

SPECIAL THANKS to **Sharyn Sanders** who contributed the majority of the photographic work for this book.

For more information on graphic designs, photo shoots, prints, or websites- contact Terrell & Sharyn Sanders

www.SeraphimStudios.net

Contact the office to Order related products
Or Shop Conveniently On-Line:

www.Rrobertwarren.com
amazon.com